DISCOVER
The
Peak District

Simon Kirwan

CONTENTS

MYRIAD

Northern Peaks

This is a vast area of moorland, an untamed landscape dominated by peat bogs and occasional gritstone outcrops or "edges". For walkers these formidable uplands provide true solitude within easy reach of Manchester and Sheffield. This is the true "dark peak", dominated by brooding peat moorlands such as Kinder Scout and Bleaklow and famous for its rugged countryside around Mam Tor and Lose Hill. The Ladybower and Woodlands valleys are famed for their beautiful reservoirs, while pretty villages such as Castleton and Hathersage provide plenty of attractions for visitors.

◀**Peveril Castle** Built in 1080 by William Peverel, one of William the Conqueror's most trusted allies and reputed to be his illegitimate son, Peveril Castle is perched above Cavedale, overlooking Castleton. The sheer sides of Cavedale helped make the castle impregnable; its role was to defend the royal hunting grounds and the local leadmining industry. In the 1170s Henry II built the keep. By Tudor times the castle had declined, although the keep continued to be used as a court-house. From Peveril there are breath-taking views over the surrounding countryside towards Mam Tor and north over the fields around Castleton towards Lose Hill.

◀▲**Castleton** Situated at the western end of the broad Hope valley this picturesque village is one of the most popular destinations in the Peak District. It is surrounded on three sides by the looming hills of Mam Tor, Hollins Cross and Lose Hill. From the west the road runs through Winnats Pass, a dramatic narrow limestone gorge. Close by are the four show caverns of Speedwell, Blue John, Treak Cliff and Peak Cavern. The mainly 17th century church of St Edmund (left) was heavily restored in 1837 but the arch dates from the Norman period. Castleton's square (above) is surrounded by fine old houses and cottages including a youth hostel and The George inn. The unusual Celtic cross on the green is the village war memorial.

▲Mam Tor The rounded contours of Mam Tor – "the Mother Mountain" – are formed from an unstable mix of sandstone and shale. The entire hill is gradually slipping into the valley giving the peak its other name of the "shivering mountain". The view above is of the spectacular eastern face of the hill. The track (right) that connects the 1700ft (518m) summit to that of Lose Hill to the north is now maintained and paved with limestone.

◄Winnats Pass A zig-zagging path brings the walker up onto the spectacular limestone gorge which overlooks Winnats Pass. This is the only route for vehicles out of the head of the Hope valley. The road climbs to 1300ft (396m) through a spectacular narrow gorge hemmed in by high limestone cliffs on either side. This lonely spot is the source of many stories and local legends. At the lower end of the pass is Speedwell Cavern, where visitors can journey to ancient mineworkings by boat just as miners did when the seams were being worked.

▲**Lose Hill** From Castleton there is an enjoyable 6.5 mile (10km) walk that takes in Lose Hill and Winnats Pass. Walkers cross the Hope valley to the gradually swelling shape of Lose Hill, which rises to 1560ft (476m). At the summit a stone waymarker (below) gives information about the surrounding scenery. The route south-west traverses Barker Bank and there are wonderful views of Mam Tor (above). The walk goes full circle taking in Peveril Castle on the way and returning weary walkers to Castleton in time for tea.

▲**Bamford** Nestling beneath the cliffs of Bamford Edge, the village of Bamford occupies an attractive position on the banks of the river Derwent close to the dams of the Upper Derwent valley. The 18th century cotton mill (above) closed down in the 1960s and now houses apartments. The mill wheel survives, and the adjoining mill pool is one of the prettiest spots along the Derwent. The church of St John the Baptist has an interesting design featuring a slim tower and a tall spire. Bamford lies on the old Sheffield to Manchester turnpike, and the Mytham bridge tollgate – just below the station – has recently been refurbished.

▶**Hope** The village of Hope is sited at the confluence of Peakshole Water and the river Noe, below Win Hill and Lose Hill. Hope is justly famous for the craftsmanship and ingenuity of its annual well-dressings which take place in July. These decorations are made by covering large boards with damp clay and then attaching petals, bark and other natural objects to make an attractive picture. The fine parish church of St Peter dates back to the early 14th century. It has a squat square tower topped by a spire. Inside there are two stone coffin lids bearing the motifs of royal huntsmen.

Stanage Edge Lying on the western moors with views over the Derwent valley, Stanage (literally "stone edge") is the largest and most impressive of the Peaks' gritstone edges and is visible from far down in the Hope valley. The entire edge is approximately 3.5 miles long from its northern tip to the southern point near the Cowper Stone. The highest point is High Neb which reaches a height of 1502ft (458m). In winter much of Stanage Edge is often snowbound. It is an ideal spot for climbing, since some of the rockfaces reach a height of 82ft (25m).

The Pennine Way The little village of Edale marks the start of the Pennine Way, Britain's first long-distance footpath which continues for 250 miles northwards. The path joins the Pennine Ridge, passes through the Yorkshire Dales, continues up into Northumberland and eventually ends at Kirk Yetholm in the Scottish Borders. It takes a fit walker about 16 days to complete the journey. By tradition, before embarking on the trek north, walkers call in at the Old Nag's Head (below). From Edale the Pennine Way winds through Grindsbrook Clough before climbing to Kinder Scout which, at 2088ft (636m), is the highest point in Derbyshire. Large parts of the Pennine Way are paved with flagstones because of their dangerous bogs. Edale – a collection of the six small hamlets of Edale, Netherbooth, Ollerbooth, Upper Booth, Barber Booth and Grindsbrook Booth – became a centre for walking when the railway which linked Manchester to Sheffield arrived in 1894.

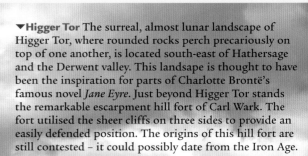

Higger Tor The surreal, almost lunar landscape of Higger Tor, where rounded rocks perch precariously on top of one another, is located south-east of Hathersage and the Derwent valley. This landsape is thought to have been the inspiration for parts of Charlotte Brontë's famous novel *Jane Eyre*. Just beyond Higger Tor stands the remarkable escarpment hill fort of Carl Wark. The fort utilised the sheer cliffs on three sides to provide an easily defended position. The origins of this hill fort are still contested – it could possibly date from the Iron Age.

▼▶Kinder Scout The windswept 15-mile wide plateau of Kinder Scout is a desolate mix of wind and ice-shattered boulders, peat bogs and deep trenches called "groughs". Located midway between Manchester and Sheffield, it is a great attraction for walkers and lovers of challenging upland terrain. The name Kinder Scout derives from the Saxon words for "water over the edge" and nowhere is this more appropriate than at Kinder Downfall (above) on its north-western edge where much of the plateau's water gathers to drop 98ft (30m) on to the land below. Doctor's Gate (below) is a bleak spot which is named after John Talbot, vicar of Glossop, who built this track to link Sheffield and Glossop.

▶▼ Ladybower Together with the Derwent and Howden, the Ladybower is one of three reservoirs built in the Upper Derwent valley to supply water to Sheffield, Derby, Nottingham and Leicester. It was constructed between 1935 and 1943 and submerged the villages of Derwent and Ashopton; much of the stone used to reinforce the dam came from houses in Derwent. The view (below) looks southeast down the eastern spur of Ladybower from the Snake Pass. The photograph (right) looks south down the upper spur of the Ladybower; it was taken from a parking spot just north of the memorial which marks the practice runs of the Dambusters before their daring wartime raids on the Möhne, Sorpe and Eder dams in the Ruhr.

▲Hayfield Overlooked by the bulk of Kinder Scout, Hayfield sits on a Roman road and old packhorse route. The many three-storey weavers' cottages in the village were built when Hayfield was a centre for cotton and wool spinning. In 1932 this was the site of the "Mass Trespass" when hundreds of ramblers set out from Bowden Bridge Quarry onto Kinder Scout to challenge the authority of landowners who restricted access to the open moorland.

▲▶Bradfield To the north-west of Sheffield this Yorkshire Peak village is divided into Low Bradfield and High Bradfield. Low Bradfield was largely destroyed in the Great Sheffield Flood of 1864. This was caused when the dam wall of Dale Dyke Dam, a recently built reservoir, broke and millions of gallons of water surged down the Loxley valley towards Mallin Bridge and Hillsborough. More than 270 people died and over 400 houses were destroyed. The church of St Nicholas (above) which stood close to the dam survived remarkably unscathed. Three headstones in the graveyard commemorate victims of the flood. By the main gate is an irregular-shaped watch house, built to protect the churchyard from grave robbers who would steal corpses for medical studies. Opposite the Old Horns Inn stands the remains of the administrative block of the old workhouse (right), built in 1769 to house the poor of the parish.

Central Peaks

The central region of the Peak District is often described as the White Peak due to the prominence of limestone. This area has a much gentler landscape than the northern Peaks. It contains the elegant spa town of Buxton and the pretty villages of Tideswell and Ashford-in-the-Water. The historic "plague village" of Eyam was immortalised by its inhabitants who, in 1665, went into quarantine so that neighbouring villages would be safeguarded from the ravages of the bubonic plague which was sweeping the country that year.

Buxton Since Roman times Buxton has been a place of pilgrimage for those seeking cures for their ills, but it was not until the late 18th century that the town came into its own as a fashionable spa. The Old Hall Hotel (right) is reputed to be the oldest hotel in England. It occupies the site of the former townhouse of Bess of Hardwick and her husband the Earl of Shrewsbury.

The Royal Devonshire Hospital, which boasts the largest unsupported dome in the country, was converted from the Stables, once used to accommodate the horses of spa visitors. It is now part of the University of Derby.

Pavilion Gardens At the heart of Buxton are the Pavilion Gardens, a beautiful 23 acre site designed in 1871 by landscape gardener Edward Milner. The Gardens are home to the impressive concert hall known as the Octagon (below) and the famous Edwardian opera house. Adjoining the Octagon is the Paxton Suite.

▲▶Hassop Three miles north of the market town of Bakewell, the tiny village of Hassop grew up around the local lead-mining industry. The imposing Hassop Hall (above) was re-built in its current form in the early 17th century on the site of a much older house owned by the Eyre family, whose wealth came from leadmining. The Eyres were devout Catholics; during the Civil War in 1643, the hall was established as a Royalist gar-rison by Roland Eyre. The church of All Saints (right) was designed as a private chapel for the Eyre family in the Classical style by the Catholic architect Joseph Ireland in 1818. The church is in the style of a Greek temple and has an impressive portico and barrel-vaulted interior.

▲Great Longstone The twin villages of Great and Little Longstone sit beneath Longstone Edge just east of Hassop. St Giles church (above), hidden away at the end of the village, dates back to the end of the 13th century. A fine beamed roof was added to the church in the 14th and 15th centuries, before the large-scale restoration in 1872 by the eminent architect Richard Norman Shaw. Inside there is a memorial to Dr Edward Buxton who tended the village during an outbreak of typhus.

◀Monsal Dale "The valley is gone – and now every fool in Buxton can be in Bakewell in half an hour and every fool at Bakewell in Buxton." This was the reaction of the eminent Victorian critic John Ruskin who campaigned against the construction in 1863 of the viaduct which carried the Midland Railway across the river Wye at Monsal Dale. The Dukes of Devonshire and Rutland also opposed the building of the line since it came too close for comfort to their estates. Modern-day reactions are quite different and the views of the river winding through Upperdale from Monsal Head and of the viaduct itself are now regarded as some of the most beautiful and popular vistas in the Peak District. A number of weirs along the river's length add to the delights on offer to walkers following the nine-mile Monsal Trail. The trail follows the course of the old railway line and runs from the Coombs Road viaduct, about one mile south of Bakewell, to Blackwell Mill junction, three miles from Buxton.

▼Monsal viaduct The Midland Railway line between Matlock and Buxton survived for just over a century, from 1863 to 1968. The five-arched viaduct which carried the railway over the river Wye is a superb example of Victorian engineering. Now owned by the Peak District National Park, it is the centre-piece of the picturesque Monsal Trail which passes through the villages of Litton and Cressbrook. Walkers will appreciate the wonderful views from the viaduct; the little bridge over the river is a great spot from which to look back and admire the Victorian architecture of the viaduct.

▲**Tideswell** A few miles north-west of Litton, on the river Wye, Tideswell is one of the Peak District's most ancient settlements. It dates back to pre-Roman times and was granted its market charter in 1251. The prosperity of Tideswell was founded on lead-mining; in the 19th century it became a centre for the textile industry, producing both cotton and silk goods.

▶**Litton** The 17th and 18th century stone cottages of Litton are clustered around the village green with its stocks and ancient cross. Litton flourished as a centre of stocking-making in the 18th century; Litton Mill, built in 1762, is now a ruin and stands as a monument to the many orphans who toiled there in appalling conditions. Unlike the mill at nearby Cressbrook, Litton Mill was notorious for the poor treatment of its young workforce, largely made up of orphans and paupers.

◄**Cressbrook** The lofty crag of Peter's Stone (left) stands guard over Cressbrook Dale, a beautiful limestone dale north of the village of Cressbrook. This village, once the site of a busy mill, is now a quiet backwater on the river Wye.

▲**Miller's Dale** The river Wye was once the source of power for Litton and Cressbrook Mills. The river has to negotiate a barrage of natural obstacles with mill races and weirs where the power of the water was diverted to drive the mill machinery.

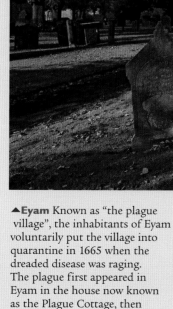

▲**Eyam** Known as "the plague village", the inhabitants of Eyam voluntarily put the village into quarantine in 1665 when the dreaded disease was raging. The plague first appeared in Eyam in the house now known as the Plague Cottage, then occupied by a travelling tailor who inadvertantly introduced the plague to Eyam in a parcel of flea-infested cloth from London. The rector of Eyam, William Mompesson, persuaded most of the inhabitants to stay and seal off the village even though many later died from the disease. The church of St Lawrence contains artefacts including Mompesson's chair; the churchyard is the resting place for many of the victims, including Mompesson's wife Catherine.

▶▼Ashford-in-the-Water

Two miles north-west of Bakewell, Ashford is a surprisingly quiet and idyllic village on the river Wye. Although lead was mined in the area until the late 19th century, Ashord is most famous for the so-called Black Marble, an impure form of limestone which turns black when polished. First quarried in 1748 by Henry Watson, the black marble was loved by the Victorians who used it in fireplaces, vases and jewellery. Some fine examples can be seen in the great limestone church of the Holy Trinity. Many of the stone cottages in the village served as workshops for its production, before a larger marble factory was established by Henry Watson. In the middle of the village is a green called Hall Orchard, once the grounds of a medieval hunting lodge. Between Hall Orchard and the river stands a 17th century tithe barn which is now a private house. Close by is the great limestone church of the Holy Trinity. The church has a fine black marble table and a plaque to Henry Watson, the founder of the local marble works.

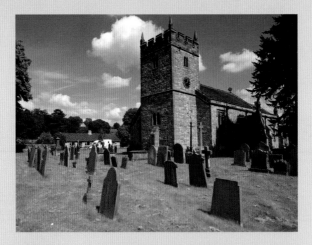

▼▶Chelmorton

Four miles south-east of Buxton, Chelmorton is 1200ft (366m) above sea level and is the highest village in Derbyshire. The steep hill of Chelmorton Low looms above the village from which a stream flows down bearing the name of Illy Willy Water. Parts of the church of St John the Baptist date back to Norman times, although the spire was added to the 13th-century tower in the 15th century. Chelmorton retains many medieval strip farms in the fields around the village, and some of the 13 surviving strips are visible in the photograph on the right. Most strip farming of this type has long since disappeared to make way for modern agriculture with its much larger fields. However, the land in Chelmorton was considered to be of such poor quality that the medieval field pattern has remained to this day.

◀Sheepwash Bridge

Close to the church, this medieval three-arched bridge is a favourite with visitors. A small enclosure nearby gives a clue to its name – sheep were flung into the river from the bridge to clean their fleeces before shearing. There are two other bridges in Ashford, one of which bears the inscription *M. Hyde 1664*, a reference to a local clergyman who was thrown from his horse and drowned in the river.

▲**Sheldon** A stone's throw from Bakewell, Sheldon was once the centre of a thriving lead-mining industry where rival gangs competed ruthlessly for the best veins of ore: today it is a sleepy village of stone cottages and farms. The Magpie Mine (above), half a mile south of the village, is one of the best preserved leadmines in Britain and has a distinctive Cornish-style engine house and chimney. The mine operated for 300 years but finally closed in 1924. It was the scene of the notorious Magpie Murders in 1833 when three miners were killed by fires started deliberately by a rival gang in a dispute over ownership of a mine. Rumour has it that the widows of the dead men cursed the mine and that the ghosts of the miners haunt the old workings today.

Eastern Peaks

This is an area of contrasting scenery, where pretty villages and historic market towns nestle in the folds of remote moors beneath spectacular escarpments or "edges". The eastern Peaks played a pivotal role in the Industrial Revolution; the Derwent Valley has been given World Heritage Site status in honour of this history. The region is also the heartland of Derbyshire's grand country houses with Chatsworth and Haddon Hall among its gems.

▲▶**Haddon Hall** The romantic and mysterious Haddon Hall is situated next to the river Wye south of Bakewell. It is one of the finest medieval and Tudor houses in England and has been the home of the Manners family, the Dukes of Rutland, since 1567. The air of romance that lingers around the house is in part due to the legend that in 1558 Lady Dorothy Vernon eloped from the house on horseback with Sir John Manners.

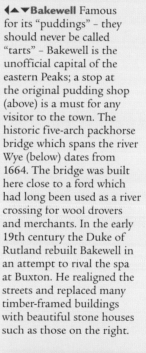

Bakewell Famous for its "puddings" – they should never be called "tarts" – Bakewell is the unofficial capital of the eastern Peaks; a stop at the original pudding shop (above) is a must for any visitor to the town. The historic five-arch packhorse bridge which spans the river Wye (below) dates from 1664. The bridge was built here close to a ford which had long been used as a river crossing for wool drovers and merchants. In the early 19th century the Duke of Rutland rebuilt Bakewell in an attempt to rival the spa at Buxton. He realigned the streets and replaced many timber-framed buildings with beautiful stone houses such as those on the right.

▲▶▼**Chatsworth** Often referred to as "the Palace of the Peak", the present house at Chatsworth is the creation of the first Duke of Devonshire who, between 1686 and 1707, re-modelled the original house and turned it into a fabulous Palladian mansion. Chatsworth is a treasure house of works of art and antiques; its superb parkland setting was achieved by the 18th century gardener Lancelot "Capability" Brown who swept away the formal gardens and created today's open, natural-looking land-scape. The grand Stable Block (below) was designed by the architect James Paine. One of the most popular garden features is the Cascade (right), a set of 24 steps over which water flows down a vertical drop of 200 feet.

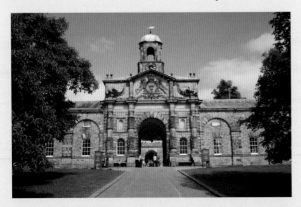

◀▼Curbar & Baslow Edge
The imposing Peak edges are at their most spectacular north of Bakewell where Froggatt's Edge, Curbar Edge and Baslow Edge join together and overlook the Derwent valley. The photograph (left) is of one of the imposing cliff faces of Baslow Edge whilst the bottom view is from Curbar Edge up the Derwent valley.
▼Calver This seven-storey former mill (middle left), which dates back to the 18th century, was used as the setting for Colditz Castle in the 1970s television series.

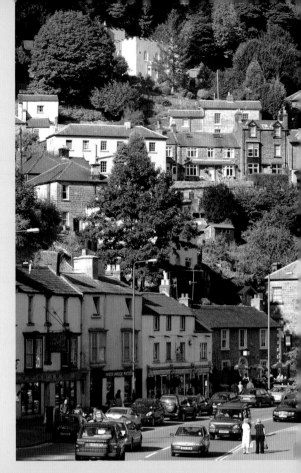

▲▶▼**Matlock** The development of Matlock and Matlock Bath as an important spa is due to the flair of the businessman John Smedley. He saw the town's potential as a hydro to rival other British and Continental towns, where ailing Victorians would come to "take the waters". The view (below) is over the town of Matlock, dominated by the vast Hydro built by Smedley in 1853. It functioned as a spa until the 1950s; today it is home to the county offices and Derbyshire Dales borough council. Matlock remains a prominent tourist resort and some of the glorious spa buildings have been beautifully refurbished, including the domed Royal Pavilion (above); built in 1910 it was at the centre of the spa complex at Matlock Bath and is now the Peak District Mining Museum. Wooded slopes rise above the busy North Parade in Matlock Bath (right). In its heyday as a spa resort, the steep valley sides were packed with fine hotels for visitors.

▲**Masson Mill** In 1783 Sir Richard Arkwright constructed a huge mill on the Derwent close to Matlock. This masterpiece is at the centre of the Derwent Valley Mills World Heritage Site which also includes the mill at Cromford, Smedley's Mill at Lea Bridge and the Silk Mill at Derby.

▲▶**Cromford** is sometimes called "the cradle of the Industrial Revolution", thanks to the legacy of Sir Richard Arkwright, the famous mill-owner who built the first successful water mill here in 1771, and the later Masson Mill which helped establish Britain's place at the forefront of the world's first Industrial Revolution. Before the arrival of Arkwright, Cromford was little more than a small hamlet consisting of a few houses and a chapel gathered around a packhorse bridge. Arkwright not only built the mill but also cottages for the workers, the Greyhound Hotel and established a market. The three-storey houses on North Street are considered to be among the finest surviving examples of industrial architecture.

South & West Peaks

Steep-sided valleys carved from exposed limestone create the startling and colourful landscape of the South Peaks. The area is bounded to the west by the river Dove and to the east by the river Derwent. Adding a special charm to the landscape is the river Wye which runs diagonally from north-west to south-east through its centre. The western Peaks are bounded by spectacular escarpments and outcrops such as the Roaches and Ramshaw Rocks.

Dovedale The Dove rises on Axe Edge and flows southwards to the edge of the Peaks. The limestone rocks on either side of the river resemble giant pieces of coral and the crags of Tissington Spires (left) are a classic example. A popular walk is from the village of Ilam along the river where first Bunster Hill and then Thorpe Cloud stand guard over the entrance to the dale. Close by is the Izaak Walton Hotel, named in memory of the author of *The Compleat Angler* in which he immortalised Dovedale.

Ashbourne Situated at the southern tip of Derbyshire, near the Staffordshire border, Ashbourne is an attractive market town with many nooks and crannies for visitors to explore. The splendid stone building (right) in Church Street housed the original Queen Elizabeth Grammar School established in 1585. The church of St Oswald was described by the author George Eliot as "the finest mere parish church in the kingdom". Ashbourne is famous, or notorious, for the annual Royal Shrovetide football game, played on Shrove Tuesday and Ash Wednesday; it often resembles a re-enactment of the Civil War rather than a sporting event.

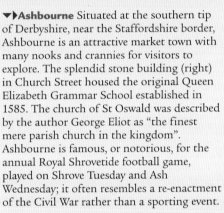

Ilam Visitors to Dovedale usually call at the pretty village of Ilam. Its distinctive appearance is due to the industrialist Jesse Watts-Russell. After the village was moved from its original position near Ilam Hall he rebuilt most of the cottages in the 1820s in a distinctive Alpine style. This explains the great distance between the village and Holy Cross church (left) which stands in the grounds of Ilam Hall. To the rear is the Chantry Chapel which contains a mausoleum to David Pike Watts, Jesse's father-in-law.

Hartington North of Alstonefield, further along the Dove valley, lies historic Hartington. This pretty settlement contains all the elements necessary for a picturesque village – a market-place, village green, duck-pond, 17th century hall, fine old church and limestone cottages. The parish church of St Giles (right) towers over the village and has a splendid Perpendicular tower. North of the village is Long Dale (above) a deserted limestone dale three miles across. Hartington is justly famous for Nuttall's Creamery. The quaint original creamery building which opened in 1876 is just off the village green and close by is the Old Cheese Shop. Manufacture of the famous Stilton cheese is now carried out in the factory on the edge of the village.

▲Alstonefield Located between Dovedale and the Manifold valley, Alstonefield contains many interesting old buildings, including an ancient tithe barn sited behind the 16th-century rectory. Next to the village green is The George, a former coaching inn and behind it is the site of the once thriving wool market.

▼Longnor On the north bank of the river Manifold, the quaint village of Longnor has become famous as the setting for the television series *Peak Practice*. The cobbled market square with its old Victorian market hall, which dates from 1873, and the network of lanes that wind around the village give Longnor a character all of its own.

▲▼Tissington Five miles north of Ashbourne, the estate village of Tissington grew up around the magnificent Jacobean Tissington Hall (above), home of the FitzHerbert family for over 400 years. Other buildings of interest include the Old School House (left), now a kindergarten. The village lays claim to being the original home of well-dressing, a tradition that dates back more than 650 years in this settlement. There are six wells in the village which are all dressed on Ascension Day.

◀▲Parwich This attractive village, situated on the high hills north of Ashbourne, is close to Dovedale and benefits from being off the beaten track. The church of St Peter appears Norman but is in fact Victorian and was built in 1873. Next to the church gate stands a beautiful limestone Celtic cross which serves as the village war memorial and honours the memory of those who fought and died in the two world wars. Above the village, Parwich Moor is home to many Bronze Age stone circles.

▶Chapel-en-le-Frith The busy market town of Chapel-en-le-Frith stands 776ft (237m) above sea level between Stockport and Buxton. The name Chapel-en-le-Frith derives from the French and means "Chapel in the forest clearing". The settlement was established as a hunting lodge in the 12th century in what was then a densely-forested area. The first chapel, built at the highest point in the town, has since been replaced by the church of St Thomas Becket. The churchyard contains the graves of many soldiers in the Scottish army who marched south in support of the Stuart king, Charles I, in 1648. The town's attractive cobbled marketplace contains stocks dating back to the Cromwellian period, together with a market cross. Church Brow is a steep, cobbled street lined with quaint stone cottages leading down from Market Street to the High Street. The Peak Forest Tramway once passed through the town and linked Bugsworth Canal Basin, at the head of the Peak Forest Canal, to the limestone quarries at Dove Holes Dale. The tramway was a busy network of horse-drawn wagons running on rails. Today the tramway is an historic trail which is steeped in the history of limestone and the factories associated with its production.

▲**Windgather Rocks** Part of the escarpment which includes Shining Tor and Goyt's Bridge, Windgather Rocks is a grit-stone crag on the Derbyshire-Cheshire border north-east of Macclesfield. Popular with trainee rock-climbers, a circular walk from the Cat & Fiddle takes in all the best features of the escarpment. There are excellent views across the Cheshire Plain and the radio telescope at Jodrell Bank can often be seen. From Windgather Rocks it is possible to walk down to the Fernilee Reservoir and then on to Fernilee dam, along the edge of a forest path. The beautiful name of Windgather derives from the Victorian mania for christening every outcrop and cave they discovered and most walkers have found that this poetic name is particularly appropriate.

▲**The Cat & Fiddle** Located on the Macclesfield to Buxton road, the historic Cat & Fiddle inn (above) stands at over 1690ft (515m) above sea level. It is reputed to be the second highest pub in Britain.

◄**Wildboarclough**
The superb terrace called Edinboro Cottages (left) is situated near Wildboarclough, a hamlet south-east of the Macclesfield Forest.